Respecting Diversity

Anti-Bias Learning: Social Justice in Action

By Emily Chiariello

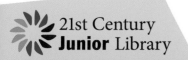

21st Century
Junior Library

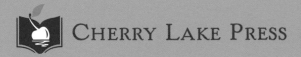
CHERRY LAKE PRESS

Published in the United States of America by Cherry Lake Publishing Group
Ann Arbor, Michigan
www.cherrylakepublishing.com

Developed with help from Learning for Justice, a project of the Southern Poverty Law Center. With special
    thanks to Monita Bell and Hoyt Phillips.
Reading Adviser: Beth Walker Gambro, MS, Ed., Reading Consultant, Yorkville, IL

Photo Credits: © Rawpixel.com/Shutterstock.com, cover, 1, 16; ©View Apart/Shutterstock.com, 4;
    ©Perry Correll/Shutterstock.com, 6; ©Monkey Business Images/Shutterstock.com, 8; ©Amir Bajric/
    Shutterstock.com, 10; ©Prostock-studio/Shutterstock.com, 12; ©Marko Rupena/Shutterstock.com, 14;
    © Viktoriia Hnatiuk/Shutterstock.com, 18; © Natalia Deriabina/Shutterstock.com, 20

Cherry Lake Press is an imprint of Cherry Lake Publishing Group.

Library of Congress Cataloging-in-Publication Data has been filed and is available at catalog.loc.gov

Cherry Lake Publishing Group would like to acknowledge the work of the Partnership for 21st Century Learning,
a Network of Battelle for Kids. Please visit http://www.battelleforkids.org/networks/p21 for more information.

Printed in the United States of America
Corporate Graphics

CONTENTS

Our world is made up of a rainbow of different kinds of people.

A Diverse World

*I like knowing other people, and I treat each person with **respect**.*

Look all around you—at the people in your classroom, your community, your country. Look at our big, beautiful world! Our world is **diverse**. There are so many different people and groups of people, each with their own identity.

Diversity means variety. When we're talking about people, diversity means there are many different kinds of people.

There are lots of different types of girls in this Girl Scout troop,
but they're probably all about the same age, from the same area,
and enjoy scouting activities.

Meeting and getting to know other people are important parts of life. We teach each other new things, make one another laugh, and help each other solve problems. Sometimes, we even become close friends!

Have you ever met someone and found out that you share things in common? Or maybe you **discover** some ways that you are different. Usually, it's a little bit of both. We are both similar to *and* different from other people.

Being the same and different are both okay ways to be. You can show respect for other people by accepting and appreciating the ways they are different from you. Differences are what make people special.

Have you had dinner with or celebrated a holiday with a friend's family? What was similar to what your family does? What was different?

Similarities and Differences

I can talk about how I am the same as and different from other people.

Another way of showing respect for diversity is learning how to talk **accurately** about our similarities and differences. We can use **knowledge** and words to let others know that we understand and appreciate who they are.

Shana, Yunus, and Kadir are the same age and in the same class. Shana is Jewish, and Yunus and Kadir

There are many different religions practiced in the
United States, and many people practice no religion at all.
Do you and your friends share the same religion?

are Muslim. They spend time together talking at lunch and playing during recess. They've learned things about each other that they didn't know before.

For example, Shana's family goes to **synagogue** services on **Shabbat**. Yunus and Kadir both pray five times a day, and Yunus attends **mosque** on Fridays. Shana's brother Ben wears a cap called a **yarmulke** on his head. Kadir's mother wears a **hijab** around her face and head, but Yunus's mom does not.

Think!

Who is your best friend? Think of three things you share in common with that friend and three things that make you different from each other.

Remember to listen carefully to friends when
you ask about their family or culture.

Asking Questions

I want to know more about other people's lives and experiences.

Classmates Shana, Yunus, and Kadir were curious and wanted to know more about each other. So they asked questions to learn about their friends' families and **culture**.

Asking questions respectfully and listening carefully is an important part of learning about other people and respecting diversity.

People in wheelchairs enjoy all kinds of sports and activities.
It isn't fair to assume based on someone's appearance.

Natalie uses a wheelchair to move around. During gym, her class was playing basketball. Her teacher, Mr. Patterson, crouched down and quietly asked Natalie if she wanted to play. Natalie proudly told Mr. Patterson that even though she wasn't able to make a basket yet, she was really good at moving around the court and passing the ball. Yes! She wanted to play! Mr. Patterson was glad he asked, rather than **assuming** Natalie couldn't play.

Make a Guess!

How many different languages do you think there are in the world? How many languages are spoken in the United States? Make a guess. Then ask an adult for help searching the internet for an answer.

We all look different on the outside,
but we all have big feelings on the inside.

Respecting Diversity

I feel connected to other people even when we are different.

Everybody has feelings. Respecting diversity means caring about the feelings of people, whether they are the same as or different from you.

On the school bus, kids were talking about what they did last weekend. Lisa said, "My moms took me to the zoo!"

Being a friend to someone means you're there to listen
and help when they need it. What else do friends do?

Jeffrey shouted, "What? You have two moms? Ew, that's so gross!"

But Kaitlyn turned to Lisa and said, "That's cool. Did you see the pandas? They're my favorite!" Lisa smiled and felt better. The two friends talked the whole bus ride to school.

Ask Questions!

Find someone in your class or grade who you don't know very well. Sit with them at lunch or spend time with them at recess. Talk to them and ask them questions. Learn three things about your new friend.

What will you do to show respect for the rainbow
of different types of people all around you?

How We're Treated

I know that how we treat each other is part of who we are.

Unfortunately, not everyone always shows respect for diversity. Today and throughout history, people are sometimes treated unfairly because they are different. Think about how Jeffrey treated Lisa when he heard she had two moms. He was mean and rude.

But we can be like Kaitlyn instead! We can show each other that no matter what our differences are, we can still be friends.

Create!

Research a culture or country that is different from your own. Make a poster collage to share what you learned with your family.

GLOSSARY

accurately (AK-yuh-ruht-lee) correctly

assuming (uh-SOO-ming) believing something without asking or checking if it's true

culture (KUHL-chuhr) the way of life, ideas, customs, and traditions of a group of people

discover (dih-SKUH-vuhr) to find or learn something

diverse (dye-VUHRSS) varied

diversity (duh-VUHR-suh-tee) a variety

hijab (hee-JAHB) a cloth head covering worn by some Muslim women

knowledge (NAH-lij) information or awareness

mosque (MAHSK) a Muslim house of worship

respect (rih-SPEKT) to be considerate of someone else's beliefs or feelings

Shabbat (shuh-BAHT) the Jewish day of worship

synagogue (SIH-nuh-gahg) a Jewish house of worship

yarmulke (YAH-muh-kuh) a skullcap worn by some Jewish men

FIND OUT MORE

WEBSITES

Learning for Justice Classroom Resources—Students texts, tasks, and more

https://www.learningforjustice.org/classroom-resources

Learning for Justice—Learn more about anti-bias work and find the full Social Justice Standards framework

https://www.learningforjustice.org

Social Justice Books—Booklists and a guide for selecting anti-bias children's books

https://socialjusticebooks.org

Welcoming Schools—Creating safe and welcoming schools

https://www.welcomingschools.org

INDEX

ABOUT THE AUTHOR

Emily Chiariello is an anti-bias educator, educational consultant, and former classroom teacher. She is the principal author of the Learning for Justice Social Justice Standards. Emily lives in Buffalo, New York.